Ritual in Mind

A Memory System for
Learning Masonic Ritual Tools

Graham Chisnell

Lewis Masonic

First published 2010
This impression 2020

ISBN 978 0 85318 344 0

Published by Lewis Masonic
an imprint of Ian Allan Publishing Ltd,
Shepperton, Middx TW17 8AS.

Printed in England.

Visit the Ian Allan Publishing website at
www.ianallanpublishing.com

Contents

Author profile

Graham Chisnell learnt to fly a glider before his seventeenth birthday, became a university lecturer at the age of 25 and was appointed as the country's youngest substantive head teacher in 1998 at the age of 26 years. Since then, he has gone on to work as an education consultant leader, a research associate for the National College for School Leadership and is a Mentor-Coach trainer.

His Masonic career is, by comparison, in its infancy. He was initiated into United Industrious Lodge No. 31 in Canterbury, Kent, in 2001. Since his initiation, he has begun the journey as a floor officer towards the Chair of King Solomon. It was during his time as a Senior Deacon that Graham applied the 'five step visual memory system' to Masonic ritual, improving his ability to recall and recite ritual in the temple.

It is Graham's wish that this book will enable many brethren, who find the thought of becoming a floor officer daunting, to become confident and competent floor officers. The core benefit of this book is to prevent the natural wastage of brethren who become disenchanted with Freemasonry as they feel they cannot become fully engaged in the workings of their respective lodges because of their perceived inability to learn and enact Masonic ritual.

Acknowledgements

My thanks go to the many inspirational people I have had the delight to come across since joining the Masonic fraternity.
In particular to Gerald Lee, who is always there as a gentle and encouraging mentor both in my Masonic life and on the golf course. The brethren of Lodge No. 31 must be recognised for their support through my emergent years as a fledgling Freemason. I am also grateful for the kind words and support I have received while drafting this book from the Deputy Provincial Grand Secretary for East Kent, Lyndon Jones.

Particular thanks go to the boundless support I have from Lucy, my wife, both for her initial artistic input to this book and the limitless encouragement she has given me, coupled with the tolerance of the time I devote to Masonic life.

Ritual in Mind

Introduction

They never warned me about this! I knew as I stood outside the door of the Masonic Temple in Canterbury, awaiting my initiation into United Industrious Lodge No. 31, that as I walked through the door things were going to be unusual. I have to confess, the anticipation as I waited in the small room outside the door of the lodge was making me feel less than comfortable. When I entered the Temple, the sounds and recitations echoed from every corner of the room, disorientating, invigorating and mesmerising. I had taken my first regular step into Freemasonry. I was hooked.

The most bewildering memory for me as an Initiate was standing face to face with brethren of the lodge who were reciting the ritual. Where were the books, the prompts, the *aides-memoire* that kept the officers' place in this complex ceremony? The words were being spoken from the heart and from the mind. It did not occur to me during the ceremony that one day I would also be on the floor, and like the officers leading me through my initiation, I would also be required to memorise this ancient ritual.

I moved swiftly through to become a Master Mason and was asked by the Worshipful Master Elect to take the floor as Inner Guard. I was honoured and delighted. It was at this juncture that the reality struck me; I was being asked to learn Masonic ritual by heart. Being blessed with a woolly memory for names and play scripts, I found learning the simplest ritual a challenge. I now needed to apply a strategy to enable my mind to retain the ritual I was now expected to enact.

As a head teacher and university lecturer, I have researched and used a wide range of memory retention techniques with my students. It was, therefore, a natural progression for me to devise a way in which these memory retention techniques could be applied to my life in Freemasonry. The memory techniques I have applied to Masonic ritual have increased my capacity to retain and recall text for the simplest ritual to the more complex and lengthy recitations. By applying the techniques in this book, you will be able to build your memory into a powerful tool for Masonic ritual.

The memory techniques in this book are not my invention; I have simply applied these memory principles to the context of Freemasonry to present a system I call the five step visual memory technique. My technique for Masonic memory draws on the neurological research by Paul Maclean into how our brain retains information. The theoretical and practical skills outlined by authors such as Tony Buzan (2006) and the educational application of memory by Trevor Hawes (1996) are also worthy of a read if you are interested in developing your understanding of the variety of ways our brain functions and how it can be used to harness its memory.

This book will provide you with a strategy for recalling ritual that is efficient and enjoyable. I will demonstrate a system of visual memory hooks for the first three working tools in craft masonry. Through the use of these memory hooks, you will be able to apply the memory principles taught in this book to any Masonic text you need to memorise and recall.

The following section introduces you to the neurological principles that underpin the visual memory technique used in this book and should help you begin to acknowledge the vast capacity your brain has to retain Masonic ritual.

Memory and your amazing brain

Your brain has an unimaginable capacity to learn. Its thirst for knowledge and understanding knows no bounds. Why then do we still struggle to remember the name of a colleague, acquaintance or old friend when we meet them in an unexpected place? Surely our amazing brain with the processing power far beyond any supercomputer should be able to cope with remembering something as uncomp-licated as a name? Panic sets in as you are led to that earth-shattering moment when you have to introduce this person to your wife: "Let me introduce you to, um..." Your heart races, your face flushes as every sinew in your mind races to find a spark, a glimmer, a whisper of memory that will dig you out of this abyss you have entered. Your wife looks at you expectantly. Still nothing. Your friend looks at you expectantly. Again, nothing. Your memory has failed you. But then, in a moment of revelation something jumps in the depths of your mind. With a confident smile you turn to your wife and say, "This is John, a good friend from Canterbury Lodge. You remember we met him and his wife at the garden party last year." Relief flows through every neural pathway in your mind and you are left with a warm, smug glow.

Your brain is constantly looking for connections; it thrives on it. The relief felt in the example above when your brain finds the link it has been searching for is felt both physically and emotionally. When your brain makes connections, it releases endorphins, nature's chemical high. When your brain engages at this emotional level you feel a buzz, you feel good and your satisfied brain gives you a well-deserved pat on the back.

The key to improving your memory lies in understanding how your brain works and aligning your learning so it is palatable for your brain. To be palatable, information must be relevant to the brain, enabling it to ingest and retain information. The bonus in paying attention to your brain is that you will experience an increased number of 'learning highs' as your brain releases endorphins into your body and your ability to learn faster and recall information efficiently will increase tenfold. The following section will take you on a journey of how your brain works and how to develop your ability to learn how to learn.

The triune brain

Ask the majority of Freemasons about their formative education and you will find that learning was all about remembering facts and figures. Our brains are able to recall the date of the Battle of Hastings, the seventh planet from the sun (always an amusing one for a school boy!) and the colour order of spectral light. The modern classroom, however, is a very different place. The revolution happening in our primary schools today involves children learning how to learn; learning how to think creatively to solve problems; learning how to explain their reasoning and qualify their emotions. In short, our future generation of learners understand what type of learner they are and how their brain processes the vast amount of information that floods in through the body's five senses. By reading the following section you will start to reflect on how you learn how to learn; let us start with the *triune brain* model.

Modern advancements in neurological imaging has enabled neuro-scientists to affirm the theory of three brains, or the triune brain. This model was proposed by Paul Maclean in 1978. The *triune brain* model explains how our brain has three distinct sections.

The first section is the most primitive; this is called the *reptilian brain*. The reptilian brain deals with fight or flight decisions and protects us from harm. It is the reptilian brain that makes us move our hand sharply away from a fire or blink when a fly flashes across our vision and it tells us when we are hungry or th The reptilian brain has been proven to be active during moments of intense aggression. The reptilian brain cannot reason, it cannot think, it simply helps our basic need for survival.

The next section of the triune brain is the *limbic system*. The limbic system is wrapped around the reptilian brain and deals with processing emotions. It is the limbic system that makes us feel at ease, makes us laugh, makes us feel nervous; it deals with love and lust. This is the part of our brain that makes us feel. It is the limbic system that makes reciting ritual in the lodge temple much harder than when we practise on our own. In the earlier example of the man who forgot his friend's name, it is the limbic system that makes us panic in that raw

Ritual in Mind

moment when we need to engage our memory. Equally, if we know how to engage our limbic system effectively, we can use it to harness our memory rather than to hinder it in such moments.

The third section of the triune brain is the *neo-cortex*. The neo-cortex is wrapped around your limbic system. This is the brain that deals with complex and abstract thought; this is your thinking brain. This part of your brain is the Vulcan brain: Mr Spock would use it to deal with logical thought and all attachment to the emotional limbic system would be severed. The reality for us, unlike Mr Spock, is that our neo-cortex is linked firmly to the emotional learning potential of our limbic system. If we engage our emotions as we learn, our potential to learn increases significantly.

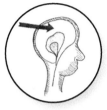

The triune brain model teaches us the importance of using our emotions when learning Masonic ritual. If we engage our limbic system while firing up our neo-cortex we are more likely to learn faster and improve our ability to recall Masonic ritual. If we engage our emotions during the learning process it is also more fun. When we engage our emotions in this way as learners we receive the treat of the endorphins flowing and the 'learning high' will leave us with a powerful incentive to revisit the learning process. We must also be aware that in order to learn efficiently, our reptilian brain must be relaxed and not feel threatened or stressed. If our reptilian brain gets a sniff that we are in a stressful situation it will, as we saw in the example of meeting our friend from the Canterbury Lodge earlier, close down our ability to learn, think and recall. As a Freemason, you need to think about the times when your reptilian brain takes over in the lodge; it is often when you are faced with reciting a freshly learnt section of ritual. Now you know your reptilian brain is there to scupper you, build a strategy to recognise the rise in emotions and block the need to fight.

Bringing your brain back to a relaxed state where the limbic system and neo-cortex are thinking and reasoning for you is paramount for memory recall and learning. In order to do this you can practise techniques that bring you back to a state of readiness to think. A simple technique is to control your breathing. Controlled breathing can bring your brain back into check during times of heightened stress and allow your brain to continue to function at its best. You will find further details on the controlled breathing technique later in the book.

Left or right brained?

Now you have lived through the trauma of splicing your brain into three constituent parts in the triune brain model let us now interrogate the processing strengths of our left and right brain. Our left brain appears to operate the right side of our body and the right brain operates the left side of our body. Recent advancements in neurological science have enabled us to take our understanding of the distinctive qualities of our left and right brain further. Our left brain deals with our logical and analytical thought process and has a factual feel about it. Our right brain enjoys creative thought; it is imaginative and deals with abstract, imaginative thought.

The left and right brain are connected by an information superhighway called the corpus callosum. The corpus callosum connects our left, logical brain with our right, creative brain. In order to be a powerful learner of Masonic ritual, we need to engage both sides of the brain and develop in particular the right brain's ability to think creatively while engaging the left brain's logical sequence and structure. The five step memory system taught in this book engages both sides of the brain; the visual images engage the right brain and the language of the ritual engage the left, making the learning process 'whole brained'. As a result, memory retention is amplified and ritual is learnt with greater ease and longevity.

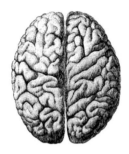

Left Brain
Language
Writing
Reading
Listening
Calculation
Logic
Analysis
Sequence

Right Brain
Creativity
Conceptual
Innovation
Idea
Image
Colour
Music/Art
Dimension
Emotion
Daydreaming

Inside the thinking brain

Your brain is bursting with brain cells, called neurons. These neurons are connected to one another by a long arm called an axon. Dendrites grow out from neurons and make links with other neurons. This linking creates a network super-highway between your neurons, and consequently between your memories.

When you think, your brain will fire across your network of brain cells to make sense of your thought. Your memories are in there somewhere. We know this is the case as a specific smell or sound can trigger a dormant memory of a place or emotion in your past. Your brain's capacity to store new memories is unlimited. With this in mind we can use the awesome power of the brain to improve our ability to memorise Masonic ritual.

Now we know how our brain works, we can use this knowledge to learn in a way that makes our brain more effective at retaining information. As we learn Masonic ritual, we can place the details of the text in compartments within our brain so we do not waste any time looking for the memory when we need it. These memory strategies use our brain's natural ability to link new learning to existing memories. It is with this strategy in mind that I use the visual link system for Masonic ritual to make learning and reciting ritual an enjoyable experience in the lodge. With the visual link system you will train your brain to take in ritual faster, recall it more readily and further enjoy your time on the floor of the lodge. You will also be able to look your DC in the eye with a smug and assured manner when he asks the fateful question, "Would anyone like to have a go at the Second Degree tools?"

Visual learning

The visual learner enjoys learning through looking. Highly visual learners will naturally use their visual skills to think and learn. Highly visual learners can have a near photographic memory and even think in colour. We all have the capacity to be a visual learner; we also have the capacity to become a better visual learner by honing our visual thinking and memory skills. This book helps improve your visual memory and will tune into your inbuilt visual memory to make learning ritual faster, more enjoyable and longer lasting. The methods I will outline are long-term memory tools, so once you have learnt the ritual, you can store this in your long-term memory and recall it at any given period.

I shall use the first degree tools as an exemplar on how to use the visual link techniques to learn Masonic ritual. You may need to spend some time practising these techniques but you will soon find that you can use the visual link techniques for all your new Masonic ritual.

The five step visual memory technique

The visual link technique both utilises your visual memory skills and with practice improves them. In order for your visual memory to improve, you need to exercise your visual abilities. The following example will allow you to develop your own strategies and enhance the capacity to improve your visual memory. Firstly, you begin with an image linked to the phrase you want to remember. The image can be in your mind's eye, or better still in front of you in the form of a doodle or picture. Now you must *power up* the image. Make the image brighter, more colourful, exaggerated: make it vibrant, sensual, humorous.

Ritual in Mind

Let us consider the phrase in the first degree tools *'knock off all superfluous knobs and excrescences'*. You may exaggerate an image by making it larger than life; imagine the gavel as a huge hammer ready to crash down on a tiny blemish on a flat surface. You can make your image vibrant by thinking of the gavel and surface in psychedelic colours or to imagine them as being blindingly white. The image becomes sensual if you imagine the feel of the gavel in your hand and the pain of it coming down mistakenly on your finger as it aims at the *superfluous knob*. To make the image humorous, you may like to imagine the finger you strike as one of your own or even your DC's. This mental work in building the image is the first step to powering up your memory for ritual.

This book introduces you to the first steps in developing a visual memory technique to improve your Masonic memory. Have a go at developing your image of the phrase *'knock off all superfluous **knobs** and excrescences'*. In selecting knob as a key word, you can build a memory of the phrase around the single image of a door knob.

Now try to draw your own image using the principles outlined above.

Let us try another simple memory image of your own. Imagine the phrase in the first degree tools *'and the C is to further prepare the surface of the stone'*. Think of all the relevant images that spring to mind in this phrase and focus on one image. Now make the image exaggerated, make it vibrant, make it sensual and make it humorous. Now close your eyes and imagine the image in your mind's eye. Introduce as much colour as you can. Now have a go at drawing the image as you imagine it.

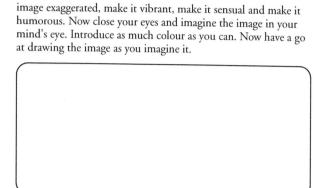

The image you draw is a representation of the image you imagine in your head and this in turn will link to the phrase that stimulated the image. As your memory forms, the image will no longer spring from the phrase, but rather act as the memory link to the phrase in your mind. This is the first step (of course with the left foot!) into this five step visual link memory technique.

The example of the first degree tools below has a range of suggested images but you are welcome to develop your own images. The key to the visual memory technique is to capture an image and link it to a phrase in the ritual. This link builds a meaningful connection between neurons in your brain and, when repeated, binds that link in your long-term memory. With practice, the technique becomes faster and easier to use. The technique will prove invaluable as you start your Masonic journey towards the vast memory requirements you will need to draw upon as Master of the lodge. Let us now take you through the visual memory technique's five steps to a more powerful Masonic memory.

So how is it done? The five step visual memory technique is simple. Start with the linked image and text, either using the suggested images below or your own preferred image. Recite the ritual with the images alongside to link the phrases and images in

Ritual in Mind

your short-term memory making the images grow in your mind by making them exaggerated, vibrant, sensual and humorous. Then try reading the words only and recall the image for each phrase. Once you have learnt the images, transfer to the image only by covering up the text. The final step is to close your eyes and imagine the images in sequence, using the images as a prompt to the ritual text. Your long-term memory will engage by this point and with practice you will fix your memory of the ritual; as a result, your recall in the lodge will be sharp and dependable.

Let's go through the five step visual memory technique one more time:

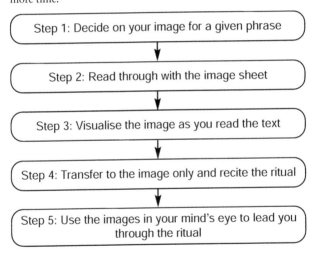

Step 1: Decide on your image for a given phrase

Step 2: Read through with the image sheet

Step 3: Visualise the image as you read the text

Step 4: Transfer to the image only and recite the ritual

Step 5: Use the images in your mind's eye to lead you through the ritual

It's that simple. With practice you will become increasingly efficient at using this technique to power up your Masonic memory.

Now it is time to begin the journey towards enjoying the full power of your memory in learning and retaining Masonic ritual. Here is how we are going to use the five step visual memory technique with the first degree tools.

Step 1: Decide on your image for a given phrase

I have created visual memory hooks for you to practise on. These are in outline so you can colour or add to the image to make it your own; alternatively feel free to be creative and invent your own visual images. Your own ideas will always be more meaningful to you and therefore act as a more potent memory glue. Give it a go and enjoy your first steps towards a powered up Masonic memory.

Step 2: Read through with the image sheet

I have created the images for the first degree tools so you can jump straight to Step 2 in the five step visual memory technique. Focus on the images as you read the text. Repeat this a number of times until the individual phrases start to sink in. Colour in the images and make them your own. This will really help your brain to make a link with them as you tune in your kinaesthetic or movement memory. When you feel ready, move to step 3.

Step 3: Visualise the image as you read the text

Cover the images and read the phrases, imagine the images popping into your mind in sequence, see the colour, the texture, the composition of the image in your mind's eye and remember the sequence of images as you read.

Step 4: Transfer to the image only and recite the ritual

Now it is time to try to memorise the images for the first degree tools.

Ritual in Mind

First degree tools

I now present to you the WT of an EA FM. They are

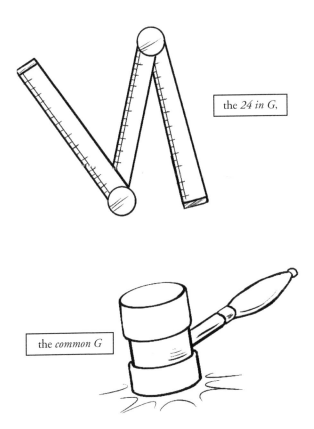

the *24 in G*,

the *common G*

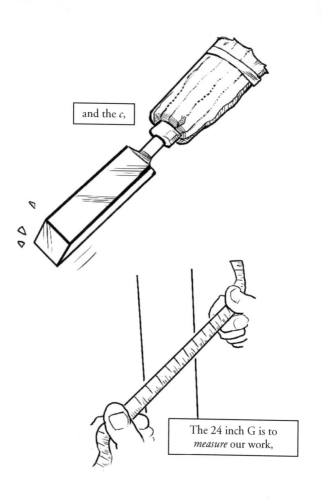

and the *c*,

The 24 inch G is to *measure* our work,

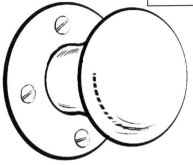

the common G to knock
off all superfluous *knobs*
and excrescences,

And the C to further smooth
and prepare the *stone*

and render it fit for the hands of the more expert *workman*.

But as we are not all Operative Masons but, rather, Free and Accepted or Speculative, we apply these Ts to our *morals*.

Ritual in Mind

In this sense, the 24 in G represents the *24 hours of the day.*

Part to be spent in *prayer* to Almighty God,

part in labour and *refreshment,*

and part in *serving a friend* or Bro in time of need without detriment to ourselves or connections

Ritual in Mind

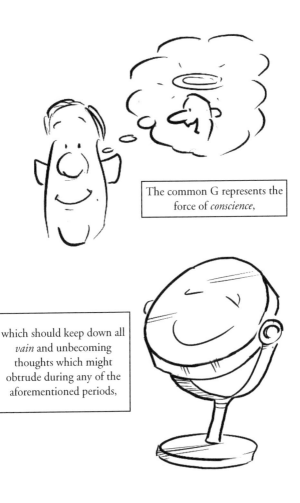

The common G represents the force of *conscience*,

which should keep down all *vain* and unbecoming thoughts which might obtrude during any of the aforementioned periods,

so that our words and
actions may ascend unpolluted
to the *Throne* of Grace.

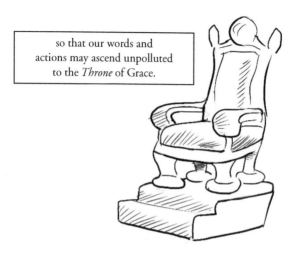

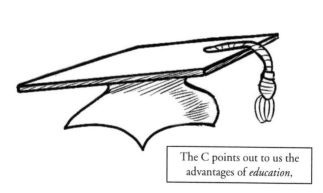

The C points out to us the
advantages of *education*,

by *which* means alone
we are rendered fit
members of regularly
organised society.

Now put your memory to the test. Here are the visual memory
hooks for the first degree tools. Now transfer to the image only
and recite the ritual using the visual memory hooks to guide your
words.

> Step 5: Use the images in your mind's eye to lead you
> through the ritual

Finally, once the sequence of images is in your mind's eye, you
can transfer to Step 5 and use your mental map of images to lead
you through the entire tools. Once you have practised this a few
times, the images will flow from one to another in sequence and
the words will connect with increasing ease. Before you know it,
you will have the first degree tools ready for delivery.

First degree tools

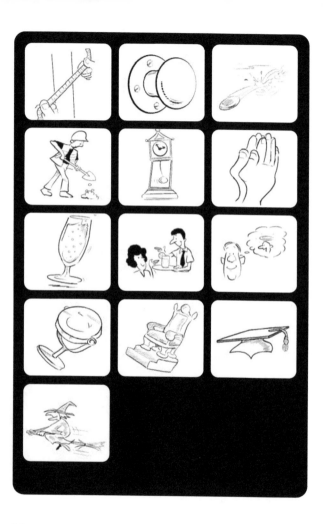

Ritual in Mind

Second degree tools

Now you have conquered the visual memory technique, we will have a go at using the skills you have learnt on the second degree tools. I have chosen the full workings of the second degree which has some wonderful imagery and great opportunities for visual memory hooks. Once again you will need to apply the five step visual memory technique to the following images.

The visual images I have selected are from my mind's eye and consequently some may not make as much sense to you as they do to me. Some images may be tenuous or may not be relevant to you. If you struggle with any of the images, simply devise your own image and you are on your way to using the five step visual memory technique to personalise your Masonic memory.

I now present to you the WT of a FCFM

They are the *S*,

the *L*

and the *PR*

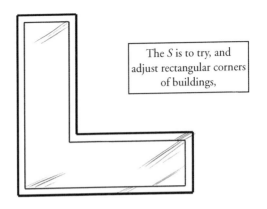

The *S* is to try, and adjust rectangular corners of buildings,

And assist in bringing *rude* matter into due form

The *L* is to lay Ls and prove horizontal

The *PR* is to try – and adjust – *uprights* while fixing them on their *proper bases*.

Ritual in Mind

But as we are not all Operative Masons, but rather Free and Accepted or Speculative, we apply these tools to our *morals*.

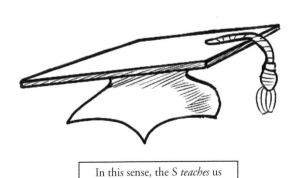

In this sense, the S *teaches* us

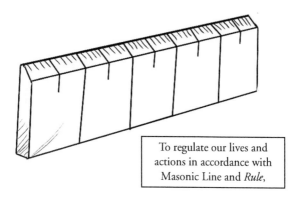

To regulate our lives and actions in accordance with Masonic Line and *Rule*,

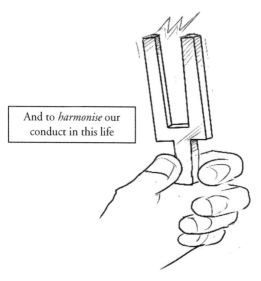

And to *harmonise* our conduct in this life

So as to *render* us acceptable

GOODNESS

To that divine being
from whom all goodness
springs

and to whom we must give an *account* of all our actions.

the *L*

Ritual in Mind

*Demon*strates

That we are all *sprung*

from the same *stock*

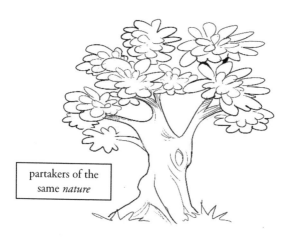

partakers of the
same *nature*

HOPE

And sharers of the same *hope*

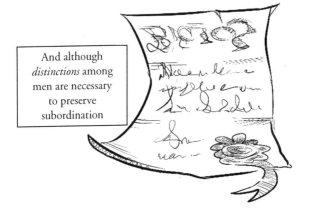

And although *distinctions* among men are necessary to preserve subordination

Ritual in Mind

Yet ought no *eminence* of situation

Make us forget that we are *bros*

Ritual in Mind

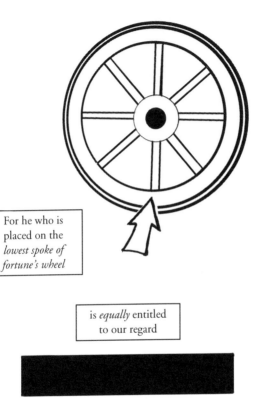

For he who is
placed on the
*lowest spoke of
fortune's wheel*

is *equally* entitled
to our regard

As a *time* will come

And the *wisest* of us knows not how soon

Ritual in Mind

When all distinctions save those of goodness and virtue shall *cease,*

GOODNESS VIRTUE

JACOB CLAIMS

and *Death,*

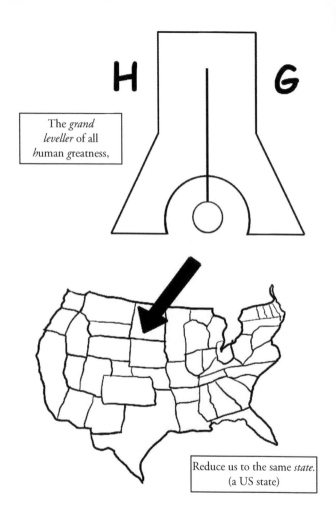

H

G

The *grand leveller* of all *h*uman greatness,

Reduce us to the same *state*.
(a US state)

The infallible
(*sounds like inflatable –*
bouncy castle)

PR,

Which like *Jacob's Ladder*
connects heaven and earth,

Is the *cri*terion (cry)
of rectitude and truth

Ritual in Mind

It *teaches* us

To *walk* justly and uprightly before *God* and *man*

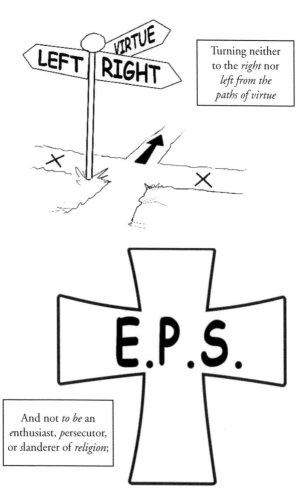

Turning neither to the *right* nor *left from the paths of virtue*

And not *to be* an *enthusiast*, *persecutor*, or *slanderer* of *religion*;

Ritual in Mind

Bending neither towards

A.I.M.R.

Avarice, injustice, malice, revenge,

Ritual in Mind   47

nor the *e*nvy and *c*ontempt of mankind

E.C. kind

But *giving up* every selfish propensity, which might injure others

Ritual in Mind

To steer the *barque* of this life *(link to tree bark)*

over the *rough seas* of passion

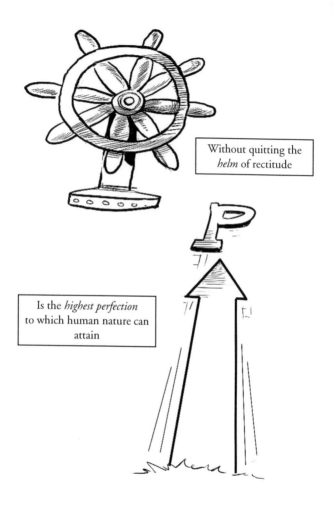

Without quitting the *helm* of rectitude

Is the *highest perfection* to which human nature can attain

Ritual in Mind

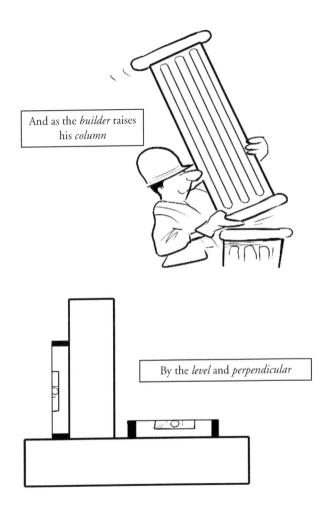

And as the *builder* raises his *column*

By the *level* and *perpendicular*

So ought every Freemason *conduct* himself towards this world

To observe a due *medium* between *a*varice and *p*rofusion

Ritual in Mind

To hold the *scales of justice* with
equal poise,

To make his *passions* and
prejudices *coincide*

With the just *line* of his *conduct*

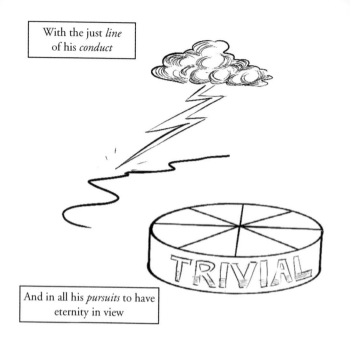

And in all his *pursuits* to have eternity in view

Thus the *S* teaches *moralit*

Ritual in Mind

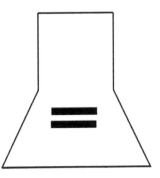

The *L* equality

and the *PR* justness and
uprightness of
life and actions;

> So that by S conduct, L steps and upright intentions we
> hope to ascend to those immortal *mansions* whence
> all goodness eminates

Now it is time to move to step four. The extended second degree working tools are the most challenging of the tools to learn, and consequently the most satisfying of the three tools when delivered well. As with the first degree tools, the images below will now become your prompt for the words within the ritual. Use the images to prompt your memory of each key phrase in the second degree tools and you will find your mind fixing the ritual in your long-term memory. You are now on your way to powering up your Masonic memory. The work you put in now will benefit you for many years to come, making the vast job of learning the ritual when on the floor of the lodge attainable and enjoyable.

> Step 4: Transfer to the image only and recite the ritual

Second degree tools

GOODNESS

£

OXO OXO

Ritual in Mind   57

Second degree tools

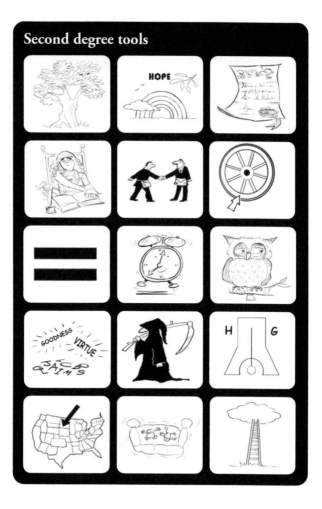

Second degree tools

Second degree tools

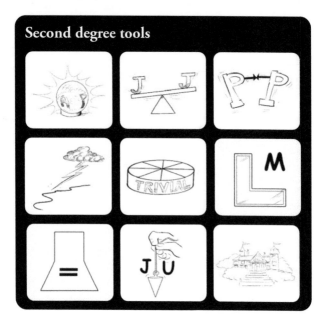

Third degree tools

I now present to you the WT of a MM. They are

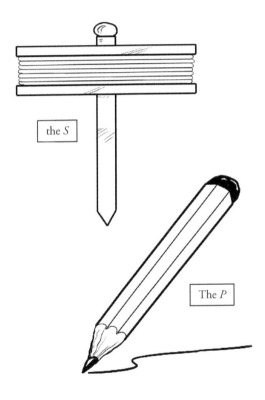

the *S*

The *P*

And the *Cs*

The S is an implement, which acts on a centre *pin*

Whence *a line is drawn* to mark out the ground for the foundation of the intended structure

Ritual in Mind

With the P the skilful *artist* delineates the building

In a draft or plan for the instruction and guidance of the *workmen*

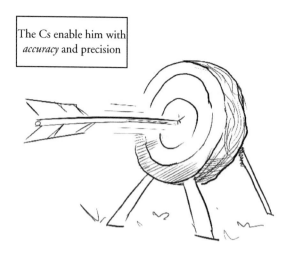

The Cs enable him with *accuracy* and precision

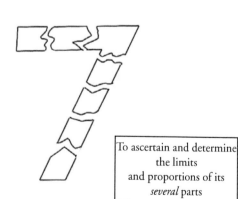

To ascertain and determine the limits and proportions of its *several* parts

But as we are not all Operative Masons, but rather Free and Accepted or Speculative, we apply these tools to our *morals*

In this sense the S points out that *straight and undeviating line* of conduct

Laid down for our *pursuit* in the VSL

The P teaches us that our words and actions are *observed* and recorded by the Almighty Architect

To whom we must give an *account* *(a count)* of all our conduct through life

Ritual in Mind

The Cs remind us of His unerring and impartial *justice*

Who, having defined, for our instruction, the limits of *good and evil*

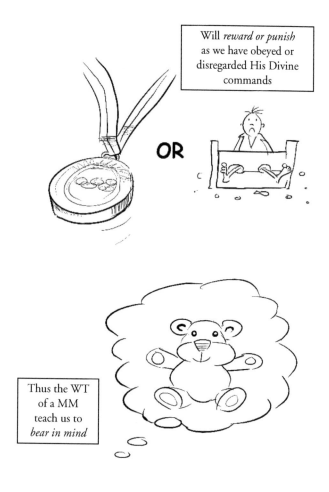

And act according to the *laws* of our Divine Creator

That when we shall be summoned from this sub*lunary* abode

We may ascend to the *Grand Lodge* above

Where the world's
Great Architect
lives and *reigns*
forever

Ritual in Mind

Third degree tools

Third degree tools

Beyond the temple

LoI gives every Freemason a chance to practise their Masonic ritual in an informal environment that is more relaxed than the temple. It is in LoI that you will be able to develop the visual memory technique as a powerful tool to improve your memory both as a participant and as an observer. I shall consider the observer first.

You are sat on the bench at LoI; the banter and discussions about Masonic ritual are echoing around the room; the DC is moving around the room, prompting, correcting and teaching. This is the time when your imaginative powers for visual memory retention are at their peak.

As you listen to the ritual being enacted, start to make visual notes for certain parts of the ceremony. You may begin with the workings of the Inner Guard. As the Inner Guard responds to the alarm and calls it a report you may jot down a ringing alarm next to three knocking knees. This visual clue reminds you that an alarm differs from a report as an alarm has more than one knock, the alarm bell ringing echoing the multiple knock of an alarm. With this visual memory image in mind, as Inner Guard you will never be confused by the difference between an alarm or a report. It is worth nothing here the variety in craft workings as a recent communication with the East Kent Provincial Deputy Grand Secretary raised; he noted that if you visit the Lodge of Harmony No. 133 in Faversham, for example, you will notice that an Alarm is one knock, so illustrating that the person wishing to enter is not aware of the correct knocks and thus 'alarming' the brethren to an unqualified admission. The memory images you create are personal to you, and at times personal to your lodge workings in particular. It is therefore necessary to emphasise that it is the process of creating your own images that will assist you in fixing the ritual in your long-term memory.

Have your notepaper to hand and jot down your visual memories as they arise; this will power up your memory to hold on to an amazing range of ritual even before you are faced with taking on the role of a floor officer. Your next step is to apply the visual memory technique to your role on the floor.

Even if you are not a floor officer you may have an opportunity to step into a floor position during LoI. In my lodge, we have 'playtime' at LoI. Playtime is where floor officer roles are mixed up and each lodge member will have been briefed to learn an aspect of a ceremony as a floor officer. Playtime provides the perfect opportunity for younger brethren to gain confidence in learning Masonic ritual. With playtime in mind, a perfect opportunity is presented for you to mention your newly found ability to recite the working tools. Your five step visual memory technique will be given a true purpose and you can take your first step in Masonic ritual learning.

As a floor officer, you will have an increasing amount of ritual workings to learn and recall. Bring along your visual memory sheet to LoI and use it to rehearse your memorised ritual. The more opportunities you have to link the image with the event of rehearsing a ceremony, the greater your capacity to fix the ritual into your long-term memory.

LoI is the perfect forum to share your newly found visual memory system with fellow brethren and share the many techniques they use to learn ritual. You will find a great deal of enjoyment by sharing your newly found five step visual memory technique and using other brethren's creativity to offer visual images that are both fun and memorable. You may also like to use some time at LoI to create a joint visual picture sequence for key ritual texts as a visual strategy in your lodge.

As you rehearse the visual memory cues, you will find the ritual seeps into your long-term memory. Once the images are fixed, you can recall them at any given point, whether rehearsing in LoI, practising in your car or engaging in your duties within the temple. The visual memory cues you make will now begin to make a real difference to the enjoyment of ceremonies and will keep your mind active during LoI and ceremonies alike.

How memory is affected in the temple

In the temple, your relaxed state is paramount to the efficiency of your memory recall. As cited earlier in the section on the triune brain, your brain must feel relaxed in order for it to recall efficiently. If your brain feels stressed or threatened the neo-cortex and limbic system will become sluggish and the reptilian brain will take over, panic will set in and every hope of a smooth recall of ritual ebbs away. The demand for recall is in its very nature a stress inducer. Place yourself back in school when your teacher demanded an answer to a times table sum. Because of the pressure of the moment, you are unable to recall the answer that when outside this stressful situation is easy to recall.

If you are to use the visual memory technique effectively, you must hold in your arsenal of effective memory strategies a range of relaxation techniques to enable your mind to work at its best. There are many techniques available to return your mind to a relaxed state and prevent your reptilian brain reverting you to a quivering mess of irrational anger or frustration. The simplest of these techniques is the controlled breathing technique.

Controlled breathing technique

This technique is used by actors to prepare themselves for the stage. The technique starts with being aware of your breathing. Start by sitting in a comfortable position. Now focus on your breaths in and out; hear them, sense your body moving, feel the movement of air in and out of your lungs. Imagine the oxygen moving around your body as you breathe in. Moving around to your extremities and into your brain. Slow your breathing down to a controlled pace, breathing more deeply and more deliberately. As you do this, you should feel the tension in your shoulders and arms release; let this happen and release the tension in your hands and legs. As you relax, you may notice your heart rate falling slightly. You will notice your senses become more alert, sounds appear louder, scents appear stronger, light appears brighter. This is a message that your brain is becoming more alert and ready to think. It is in this relaxed state that learning and recall is at its most potent. With practice you will be able to enter this state in three breaths. I have used this technique in the lodge before giving the tools; my nerves dissipate, my mind has the oxygen needed to operate at its best and my body is relaxed, making the experience enjoyable for both myself and others within the lodge.

Projected confidence technique

The projected confidence technique is a very useful strategy to use inside the lodge. It involves you playing a mind game. Simply conjure up the image of a person who you consider to be the most confident and able Mason you know. They may have a great grasp of ritual; they may have the characteristics in the lodge that exude confidence. All you have to do now is to imagine, no… more than imagine, believe, you are this person. In every sinew of your body believe you are this confident Mason, able to recall ritual, able to command attention in the lodge, able to capture people's envy and give it back as caring regard. It may be helpful to add a quality from someone you admire outside the lodge, perhaps the carefree entrepreneur attitude of Richard Branson, or the wise counsel of Nelson Mandela. If you truly believe you hold these qualities, your anxiety within the lodge will begin to dissipate, your mind will be in a confident and relaxed state and you will live up to the person you have become.

The projected confidence technique is very useful when visiting another lodge as you can use this as a means of being more confident when meeting fellow Masons and in your conversations at the festive board. If you imagine yourself as a confident conversationalist, perhaps in your mind's eye you have Michael Parkinson or Jonathan Ross, your interactions with brethren will be more enjoyable for you and them. Use the projected confidence technique to trick your mind into believing you own the lodge, and with this will come the blissful humility that arrives when you accept that in this confident state of mind, you are now equally ranked with every brother sat around you. It is this equality that is the essence of the level in the second degree tools.

Associated feeling technique

The associated feeling technique is a simple, yet effective, relaxation technique. This is used in self-hypnosis and empowers the person to recall a moment in their life where they felt calm and energised. This technique asks you to recall a moment in your life when you felt relaxed, imagine the place, the feeling, the smell, the colours; immerse yourself in the moment. Now think of a moment where you felt really energised; it may be a time when you felt exhilarated or excited or aroused. Think of that moment in all its splendour, remembering the feelings, colours, smells, sounds, tastes. You now need to bring these two moments together so your energised memory and relaxed memory act as one. Imagine the memories originating from differing sides of your brain and slowly merging. As they merge, make a 'fist' with your toes and slowly release the tension until both images are together. We use the toes as it is very difficult for anyone to see you practising this technique unless you are barefoot!

After practising this a few times, you will begin to allow your limbic system (your feeling brain) to believe it is once again in that relaxed but alert state. The consequence is that your brain will be tricked into thinking it is relaxed but will be alert and ready for recall.

Pace setting technique

It is said that the most important element of the lodge is holding in your mind the two letters 'SD'. This does not allude to the Senior Deacon, but a principle that leads every Freemason to become a confident ritualist. When reciting ritual, hold in your mind's eye the giant letters SD and tell yourself, and I mean this literally by sub-verbalising (to speak out loud in your mind), before reciting the tools… 'Slow Down'.

By slowing down you will give your brain time to feed you the ritual in bite-size chunks. Your voice will be clear and diction easy. Your heart rate will slow to match your calm delivery. And above all, your fellow brethren will listen in awe to your delivery of the tools. By consciously pacing your delivery, the visual memory technique will be empowered to do its job for you and drip feed each visual memory hook as you need it. So remember, before every delivery, imagine those giant letters SD.

Practice makes just, perfect and regular

As this book reaches its conclusion, let us reflect on the principles you have been introduced to. Your brain is an amazing tool with an unimaginable capacity to retain Masonic ritual. Your understanding of how the brain operates within the triune brain model will enable you to develop the most conducive conditions for learning the first three Masonic tools. You now know that in order to learn effectively, you must be relaxed, be well fed, be hydrated and that your visual images need to be vibrant and amusing. This knowledge will enable your brain to ingest new ritual with the greatest of ease.

The right brained learner will particularly benefit from the visual memory technique introduced in this book. The highly visual learner will be able to imagine and retain images with increasing ease as they practise the principles within the visual memory technique and, with practice, be able to use their visual memory strengths to learn and recall Masonic ritual from their long-term memory.

Understanding the thinking brain has enabled us to explore how we can learn how to learn. Memory retention is a skill that can be learnt and developed. The visual memory technique is one of a number of ways in which we can power up our memory to become more efficient in the temple. In addition to the thinking brain, this book has introduced the power of visual learning as one of three key methods (the remaining two being kinaesthetic and auditory learning) our brain uses to digest new knowledge and skills.

The book then went on to teach the five step visual memory technique as a powerful model for visual memory retention. This model was applied to the first degree tools. By actively colouring the images representing key phrases in the first degree tools, your brain began to develop its ability to store visual clues to increase the memory retention of the first degree tools. By switching from the text to visual images, or memory hooks, you are now able to store Masonic text in your long-term memory as an auditory memory (namely the sound of reciting the tools) as well as a visual memory through the use of the images in this book.

The book finally explored a range of techniques for enabling your memory to work at its optimum level when in the temple. The many distractions to your brain often reduce your ability to recall ritual. Techniques including the controlled breathing and associated feeling technique act as a physical and mental stimulus to calm your brain and blocking your reptilian brain from taking charge of your nerves and block the pathway between your memory and your mouth. The pace setting technique then reminded us of the arch enemy of good Masonic ritual, namely speaking too quickly. By recalling a giant SD prior to the delivery of the tools, every Mason who practises the techniques outlined in this book will be empowered to deliver the tools in a manner they will be proud of. This pride will be amplified as your Masonic brethren congratulate you on your delivery of the tools.

Finally, all that is left for your mastery of the five step visual memory technique and of the tools is to practise. This technique is not magical; memory does not work without effort. You must practise the skills taught in this book until your mind becomes proficient at using the technique. Once mastered, the technique becomes tacit, and operates as a learnt skill that can be applied to every aspect of Masonic ritual. Enjoy your new and improved memory.

References and Great reads in Memory and Thinking

T. Buzan (2006)	*Use Your Head: Innovative learning and thinking techniques to fulfil your potential*	BBC
T. Hawes (1996)	*Effective teaching and learning in the primary classroom*	Optimal Learning
D. Royal (2008)	*Masonic Mnemonics*	Lewis Masonic
A. Smith & N. Call (2001)	*The ALPS Approach resource book*	Network Educational Press
A. Smith & N. Call (1999)	*The AlpsApproach – Accelerated Learning in Primary Schools*	Network Educational Press

Ritual in Mind

BV - #0016 - 120821 - C0 - 148/105/5 - PB - 9780853183440 - Gloss Lamination